The Premature Burial

*Claustrophobic Nightmares,
Obsession & Terror of Living Death*

A Modern Translation
Adapted for the Contemporary Reader

Edgar Allan Poe

Translated by Tim Zengerink

Table of Contents

Preface
Message to the Reader

Rebuilding the Greatest Library in Human History

Thousands of years ago, the Library of Alexandria was the heart of global knowledge — a sanctuary where the wisdom of every known civilization was gathered and shared freely.

And then, it was lost.

Now, we're rebuilding it — and you are invited to join us.

At the Library of Alexandria, we've set out to make every book available to every person on Earth — not just in print, but in every language, every format, and for every reader.

Here's how we do it:

- **Deluxe Print Editions at True Printing Cost** - Order any book as a high-quality paperback, elegant hardcover, or stunning boxset — and only pay what it costs to print. No markups. No middlemen.
- **Unlimited Access to the Greatest Works** - Enjoy thousands of timeless classics — from Plato to Shakespeare to Tolstoy — in beautiful, modern eBook and audiobook editions. Read and listen without limits — for every reader, everywhere.
- **Modern Translations for Every Language & Dialect** - We're reimagining the classics in clear, accessible language — and translating them into every dialect imaginable. Everyone deserves to understand humanity's greatest ideas.

When you visit **LibraryofAlexandria.com**, you're not just accessing books — you're joining a global movement to restore, preserve, and share the wisdom of civilization.

Join us today at LibraryofAlexandria.com

Together, we'll ensure the light of human wisdom never fades again.

With gratitude,

The Modern Library of Alexandria Team

Visit:
www.libraryofalexandria.com
Or scan the code below:

Introduction

Poe's Exploration of Entombment, Fear, and the Gothic Psyche

Edgar Allan Poe's *The Premature Burial* (1844) is a haunting meditation on one of humanity's most primal and enduring fears: the terror of being buried alive. This story, which straddles the line between fiction and essay, is as much a psychological case study as it is a Gothic narrative. It delves into the mind of a narrator who is consumed by a pathological obsession with the possibility of premature burial—a fear that was both personal to Poe and culturally widespread in the 19th century. Through vivid descriptions, real-life anecdotes, and an unsettling exploration of the boundary between life and death, Poe crafts a work that resonates with universal anxieties about mortality, consciousness, and helplessness.

At the heart of *The Premature Burial* lies Poe's fascination with states of suspended animation—conditions where the difference between life and death becomes uncertain. In the 19th century, medical science was far less advanced than it is today, and cases of premature burial were rumored to occur with alarming frequency. Newspapers and periodicals of Poe's time often reported on individuals who were mistakenly declared dead, only to awaken in their coffins or graves. This cultural fear was amplified by the lack of reliable methods for determining death and by the era's macabre fascination with death rituals, funerals, and burial practices. Poe, ever attuned to the fears of his audience, used these anxieties to create one of his most disturbing works.

The story is structured as a blend of factual exposition and personal confession. The narrator begins by recounting various historical and contemporary cases of premature burial, describing them in chilling detail to illustrate the reality of the threat. These anecdotes, though often sensationalized, lend the story an air of authenticity, blurring the line between documented truth and fictional horror. As the narrative progresses, the focus shifts to the narrator's own experiences and psychological torment. His fear of being buried alive becomes so overwhelming that it dictates his daily life, leading him to construct elaborate safety measures and even a specialized coffin designed to prevent such a fate.

Poe's genius in this story lies not only in his ability to evoke terror but also in his exploration of how fear itself can become a form of living death. The narrator's obsession is so all-consuming that it effectively entombs him while he is still alive. His world narrows to a single point of anxiety, and his mental state deteriorates as he becomes increasingly unable to distinguish between rational precaution and pathological delusion. This psychological dimension elevates *The Premature Burial* from a mere horror tale to a profound examination of the human mind under the influence of fear.

The climax of the story arrives when the narrator, believing he has been buried alive, awakens in total darkness and confinement, convinced that his worst nightmare has come true. The intensity of this moment—described in visceral, claustrophobic detail—places the reader directly inside the suffocating terror of the protagonist's mind. When it is revealed that he is not in a coffin but in the berth of a small boat, the experience shocks him into a new understanding of his own life and mortality. This epiphany allows him to break free from his obsession, suggesting that facing one's fears directly can be a form of liberation.

Themes of Mortality, Obsession, and Cultural Fear

The Premature Burial is not just a tale of personal terror but also a reflection of broader societal anxieties about death and the reliability of medical science. In the 19th century, the line between life and death was often blurred, as medical practitioners lacked the tools and knowledge to confirm death with absolute certainty. This uncertainty gave rise to various safety devices—such as "safety coffins" equipped with bells or breathing tubes—designed to allow mistakenly buried individuals to signal for help. Poe's story captures this cultural paranoia, using it as both a backdrop and a metaphor for deeper psychological concerns.

The theme of obsession runs throughout the narrative. The narrator's fear of premature burial dominates every aspect of his life, rendering him a prisoner of his own mind. Poe portrays this obsession with remarkable psychological insight, depicting how an irrational fear, if left unchecked, can grow into an all-consuming force that robs life of its vitality and meaning. The narrator's retreat into isolation, his compulsive preparations, and his inability to think of anything beyond his fear all illustrate the destructive power of obsessive thought.

Death, as in much of Poe's work, is both a literal and symbolic presence in *The Premature Burial*. On a literal level, the story deals with the prospect of being mistakenly consigned to the grave. On a symbolic level, premature burial represents the fear of being trapped or confined, of losing agency and voice, of being silenced before one's time.

This symbolic dimension resonates with broader human fears—fear of the unknown, fear of helplessness, and fear of the inevitability of death itself.

Poe's narrative also touches on themes of rationality versus irrationality. The narrator's fear, while rooted in real historical cases, spirals into a form of madness that isolates him from normal human experience. His eventual awakening—both literal and metaphorical—can be read as a triumph of rationality over irrational fear, or as an acknowledgment of the futility of attempting to control death. This ambiguity is typical of Poe, who often presents terror not as something external but as a reflection of the human mind's darkest recesses.

Poe's Style and the Reader's Experience

Edgar Allan Poe's mastery of language and structure is evident throughout *The Premature Burial*. His prose is rich with sensory detail, drawing the reader into the suffocating confines of the coffin-like spaces he describes. The tactile imagery—of tight enclosures, stifling air, and the weight of earth above—creates an almost physical sensation of claustrophobia. Through repetition and rhythm, Poe mimics the obsessive patterns of the narrator's thoughts, allowing readers to experience his mounting dread firsthand.

The story's hybrid structure—part essay, part personal narrative—adds to its unique impact. By beginning with purportedly factual accounts of premature burial, Poe builds a foundation of credibility that heightens the horror of the narrator's personal ordeal. The blending of fact and fiction was a hallmark of Poe's style, designed to blur the boundaries between reality and imagination and to leave readers questioning what they had just read.

Poe's exploration of psychological horror is particularly sophisticated here. Unlike tales that rely on external monsters or supernatural forces, *The Premature Burial* finds its terror within the mind of the protagonist. The true horror is not the possibility of being buried alive but the way this fear dominates and distorts the narrator's entire existence. By focusing on this internal dimension of fear, Poe anticipates modern psychological horror, where the mind itself becomes the primary battleground.

For contemporary readers, *The Premature Burial* remains a deeply unsettling work. Even in an era of advanced medical science, the fear of being trapped, silenced, or misunderstood remains powerful and relatable. The story speaks to universal anxieties about losing control, about facing death alone, and about the thin line that separates life from its opposite. Poe's narrative, with its intense focus on sensory detail and psychological realism, ensures that these fears remain vivid and immediate.

As you read *The Premature Burial*, it is worth considering both its historical context and its enduring relevance. The story reflects a time when death was a constant presence and medical errors could easily lead to horrifying outcomes. Yet its deeper themes—obsession, fear, and the struggle to confront mortality—are timeless. Poe invites us not only to share in the narrator's terror but also to reflect on our own relationship with fear and death. By doing so, he transforms a tale of Gothic horror into a profound meditation on the human condition.

The Premature Burial

There are certain themes that completely captivate our interest, but they are far too horrifying to be used in legitimate fiction. Writers of romance must avoid these subjects if they don't want to offend or disgust their readers. These themes can only be properly handled when the severity and majesty of Truth give them meaning and support. We experience, for instance, the most intense "pleasurable pain" when reading accounts of the Passage of the Beresina, the Earthquake at Lisbon, the Plague at London, the Massacre of St. Bartholomew, or the suffocation of one hundred and twenty-three prisoners in the Black Hole at Calcutta. But in these accounts, it is the fact—it is the reality—it is the history that moves us. If these were fictional inventions, we would view them with nothing but disgust.

I have mentioned a few of the more notable and terrible disasters in recorded history; but with these events, it is both the scale and the nature of the catastrophe that so powerfully captures the imagination. I don't need to remind the reader that from the long and eerie catalog of human suffering, I could have chosen many individual cases filled with more genuine anguish than any of these broad categories of tragedy. The real misery, in fact—the deepest sorrow—is specific, not widespread. That the most horrifying depths of pain are experienced by individual people, and never by groups as a whole—for this we should be grateful to a compassionate God!

Being buried alive is, without a doubt, the most horrifying fate that could ever befall a human being. Those who truly consider this matter will hardly deny that such a thing has happened frequently—very frequently indeed. The line separating life from death is, at best, unclear and uncertain. Who can determine where one ends and the other begins? We understand that certain illnesses can cause a complete halt of all visible signs of life, yet these interruptions are merely temporary suspensions. These are simply brief pauses in an incomprehensible system. After a certain amount of time passes, some invisible and mysterious force restarts the magical mechanisms and enchanted workings. The silver cord had not been permanently severed, nor the golden bowl forever shattered. But during this time, where was the soul?

Beyond the logical conclusion that such causes must inevitably produce such effects—that the well-documented occurrence of these cases of suspended animation must naturally lead, from time to time, to premature burials—beyond this consideration, we have direct evidence from medical and everyday experience proving that a vast number of such burials have actually occurred. I could immediately reference, if needed, a hundred well-documented cases. One particularly striking case, whose details may still be fresh in some of my readers' memories, happened not long ago in the nearby city of Baltimore, where it caused painful, intense, and widespread alarm. The wife of one of the most respected citizens—a prominent lawyer and member of Congress—was struck by a sudden and mysterious illness that completely stumped her doctors. After considerable suffering, she died, or appeared to die. No one suspected, or had any reason to suspect, that she wasn't truly dead. She displayed all the typical signs of death. Her face took on the characteristic pinched and hollow appearance. Her lips had the usual marble-like paleness. Her eyes were dull and lifeless. There was no warmth in her body. Her pulse had stopped. For three days the body remained unburied, during which time it became rigid as stone. The funeral was rushed, in fact, because of the rapid progression of what was believed to be decay.

The woman was placed in her family tomb, which remained untouched for the next three years. When this period ended, the vault was opened to receive a coffin; but what a terrible shock awaited the husband, who personally opened the door! As the entrance swung outward, some white-clothed figure fell clattering into his arms. It was his wife's skeleton, still wrapped in her burial shroud that had not yet decayed.

A thorough investigation made it clear that she had come back to life within two days after being buried; her frantic movements inside the coffin had caused it to tumble from a ledge or shelf to the floor, where it broke apart enough to allow her to get out. A lamp that had been accidentally left behind, filled with oil, inside the tomb was discovered empty; though it could have simply run dry through evaporation. On the highest of the steps that descended into the terrifying chamber lay a large piece of the coffin, which it appeared she had used to try to get attention by banging against the iron door. While doing this, she likely fainted, or perhaps died from pure terror; and as she collapsed, her burial shroud got caught on some ironwork that stuck out from the interior. This is how she stayed, and this is how she decomposed, standing upright.

In 1810, a case of being buried alive occurred in France, accompanied by circumstances that strongly support the claim that truth is indeed stranger than fiction. The main character of this story was a Mademoiselle Victorine Lafourcade, a young woman from a distinguished family, wealthy, and possessing great personal beauty. Among her many admirers was Julien Bossuet, a poor writer and journalist from Paris. His abilities and overall charm had caught the attention of the heiress, who appeared to truly love him; however, her family pride ultimately led her to reject him and marry a Monsieur Renelle, a banker and diplomat of considerable standing. After their marriage, though, this gentleman ignored her and perhaps even treated her cruelly. After spending several miserable years with him, she died—or at least her condition resembled death so closely that it fooled everyone who observed her. She was buried—not in a tomb, but in a regular grave in the village where she was born. Overcome with grief and still consumed by memories of deep love, her former suitor traveled from the capital to the distant province where the village was located, with the romantic intention of digging up the body and taking possession of her beautiful hair. He arrived at the grave. At midnight he dug up the coffin, opened it, and was about to cut off the hair when he was stopped by the opening of her beloved eyes. The truth was that the lady had been buried alive. Life had not completely left her, and she was awakened from the deep sleep that had been mistaken for death by her lover's touch. He carried her desperately to his rooms in the village. He used certain strong remedies that his considerable medical knowledge suggested. Eventually, she came back to life. She recognized the man who had saved her. She stayed with him until she gradually regained her full health. Her woman's heart was not made of stone, and this final demonstration of love was enough to soften it. She gave her heart to Bossuet. She never returned to her husband, but instead hid her return to life from him and escaped with her lover to America. Twenty years later, the two came back to France, believing that time had changed the lady's appearance so much that her acquaintances would not be able to identify her. They were wrong, however, because at their first encounter, Monsieur Renelle actually recognized and claimed his wife. She fought this claim, and a court supported her resistance, ruling that the unusual circumstances, combined with the long passage of time, had eliminated both morally and legally the husband's authority over her.

The "Chirurgical Journal" of Leipzig, a respected and valuable periodical that some American publisher should consider translating and republishing, documented in a recent issue a very troubling incident of this nature.

An artillery officer, a man of enormous size and excellent health, was thrown from an uncontrollable horse and suffered a severe head injury that immediately knocked him unconscious; his skull was slightly cracked, but doctors didn't expect any immediate danger. The surgical procedure to relieve pressure on his brain was completed successfully. He underwent bloodletting, and many other standard treatments of the time were used. Gradually, however, he sank into an increasingly hopeless state of unconsciousness, and eventually, it was believed that he had died.

The weather was warm, and he was buried with unseemly haste in one of the public cemeteries. His funeral occurred on Thursday. On the following Sunday, the cemetery grounds were crowded with visitors as usual, and around noon an intense commotion arose from a peasant's claim that while he sat on the officer's grave, he had clearly felt the earth moving beneath him, as though someone was struggling underground. Initially, people paid little attention to the man's statement, but his obvious fear and stubborn persistence in telling his story eventually had their expected impact on the crowd. Shovels were quickly obtained, and the grave, which was disgracefully shallow, was opened within minutes enough to reveal the head of the person buried there. He appeared to be dead at that moment, but he sat almost upright inside his coffin, having partially lifted the lid during his desperate struggles.

He was immediately taken to the nearest hospital, where doctors determined he was still alive, though in a state of suffocation. After several hours, he regained consciousness, recognized people he knew, and spoke in fragmented sentences about the terrible suffering he had experienced in the grave.

From what he told them, it was obvious that he must have been aware and alive for more than an hour while buried underground, before losing consciousness. The grave had been carelessly and loosely filled with extremely porous soil, which meant that some air could get through. He could hear the footsteps of people walking above him and tried to make noise so they would hear him too. He said it was the commotion happening in the cemetery grounds that seemed to wake him from a deep sleep, but as soon as he woke up, he immediately understood the terrible horror of his situation.

This patient, according to the records, was recovering well and appeared to be on track for a complete recovery, but became a victim of questionable medical experimentation. The galvanic battery was used on him, and he suddenly died during one of those intense convulsions that the device sometimes causes.

The mention of the galvanic battery, however, brings to mind a well-known and quite extraordinary case where its use successfully restored life to a young London lawyer who had been buried for two days. This incident took place in

1831 and caused a tremendous stir wherever people discussed it.

The patient, Mr. Edward Stapleton, had died, apparently from typhus fever, along with some unusual symptoms that had sparked the curiosity of his doctors. After his apparent death, his family was asked to approve an autopsy, but they refused to allow it. As frequently occurs when such refusals happen, the doctors decided to dig up the body and examine it privately at their convenience. Arrangements were easily made with some of the many groups of grave robbers that were common in London; and on the third night following the funeral, the presumed corpse was removed from a grave eight feet deep and placed in the examination room of one of the private hospitals.

A fairly large cut had already been made in the abdomen when the fresh and well-preserved condition of the body suggested trying the electric battery. One experiment followed another, and the usual effects occurred, with nothing particularly noteworthy about them except that on one or two occasions, the convulsive movements showed an unusually lifelike quality.

The night was growing late. Dawn was approaching, and they finally decided it was time to begin the dissection. However, one student was particularly eager to test his own theory and insisted on applying the electrical battery to one of the chest muscles. They made a crude incision and quickly brought a wire into contact with the muscle. Suddenly, the patient moved with a swift but completely natural motion, rose from the table, walked to the center of the room, looked around nervously for several moments, and then—spoke. His words were impossible to understand, but he was definitely speaking; each syllable was clearly pronounced. After speaking, he collapsed heavily onto the floor.

For a few moments everyone was frozen with shock—but the urgent situation quickly brought them back to their senses. They could see that Mr. Stapleton was alive, though he had fainted. When they gave him ether, he came to and quickly recovered his health, returning to the company of his friends—though they kept the knowledge of his revival from everyone until there was no longer any fear of a setback. Their amazement—their overwhelming astonishment—can easily be imagined.

The most fascinating aspect of this incident, however, lies in what Mr. S. himself claims. He states that he was never completely unconscious—that, dimly and hazily, he remained aware of everything that happened to him, from the moment his doctors declared him dead to the moment he collapsed on the hospital floor. "I am alive," were the misunderstood words that he had tried desperately to speak when he realized he was in the dissecting room.

It would be easy to share many more stories like these, but I'll stop here because we really don't need them to prove that people are sometimes buried alive. When we think about how rarely we're actually able to discover these cases due to their very nature, we have to accept that they probably happen often without us knowing about it. In fact, whenever a cemetery is disturbed for any reason on a large scale, skeletons are almost always found in positions that raise the most terrifying suspicions.

The suspicion is truly frightening—but the reality is even more terrifying! We can say without doubt that no experience is better suited to create the ultimate physical and mental suffering than being buried alive. The crushing pressure on the lungs—the suffocating vapors from the moist soil—the way burial clothes stick to your body—the tight grip of the cramped coffin—the complete darkness of absolute night—the silence that drowns you like an ocean—the invisible but real presence of death itself—all of these things, combined with thoughts of the fresh air and grass above, memories of loved ones who would rush to rescue us if they only knew what had happened, and the knowledge that they can never find out—that our hopeless situation is the same as those who are truly dead—these thoughts, I tell you, fill a heart that still beats with such overwhelming and unbearable terror that even the boldest imagination must turn away. We know of nothing more agonizing on Earth—we cannot even imagine anything half as horrible in the deepest pits of Hell. This is why all stories about this subject hold such deep fascination; a fascination that, because of the sacred fear the topic itself inspires, depends entirely on whether we believe the story being told is true. What I am about to share comes from my own direct knowledge—from my own real and personal experience.

For several years I had been experiencing attacks of the unusual disorder that doctors have agreed to call catalepsy, lacking a more precise name. While both the immediate and underlying causes, and even the actual diagnosis, of this disease remain mysterious, its obvious and apparent characteristics are well enough understood. Its variations seem to be mainly of degree. Sometimes the patient lies, for only a day, or even for a shorter period, in a kind of extreme lethargy. He is unconscious and externally motionless; but the heartbeat is still faintly detectable; some traces of warmth remain; a slight color lingers in the center of the cheek; and, when a mirror is held to the lips, we can detect a sluggish, irregular, and wavering action of the lungs. Then again the duration of the trance lasts for weeks—even for months; while the closest examination, and the most thorough medical tests, fail to establish any meaningful distinction between the condition of the sufferer and what we understand as absolute death. Very often he is saved from premature burial solely by the knowledge of his friends that he has been previously subject to catalepsy, by the resulting suspicion this creates, and, above all, by the absence of decay. The progression of the illness is, fortunately, gradual. The first manifestations, although pronounced, are unmistakable. The episodes grow successively more and more distinct, and each lasts for a longer period than the one before. In this lies the main protection from burial alive. The unfortunate person whose first attack should be of the extreme nature which is occasionally seen, would almost inevitably be buried alive in the tomb.

My own situation was no different in any significant way from the cases described in medical textbooks. Sometimes, for no obvious reason, I would gradually slip into a state of partial unconsciousness, or semi-fainting; and in this state, feeling no pain, unable to move, or properly speaking, to think clearly, but maintaining a dim, sluggish awareness of being alive and of the people gathered around my bed, I would remain until the turning point of the illness suddenly brought me back to complete awareness. At other times the attack would strike me quickly and violently. I would become ill, and numb, and cold, and dizzy, and would immediately collapse. Then, for weeks on end, everything was empty, and dark, and quiet, and Nothingness consumed the entire world. Complete destruction could not have been more absolute. From these more severe episodes I would recover, though, with a slowness that matched how suddenly the attack had begun. Just as dawn breaks for the friendless and homeless wanderer who walks the streets through the long, barren winter night—just as slowly—just as wearily—just as hopefully did the light of the Soul return to me.

Apart from my tendency to fall into trances, my overall health seemed to be good. I couldn't tell that it was affected at all by the widespread illness—unless you could consider a peculiarity in my normal sleep as something caused by it. When I woke up from sleep, I could never immediately regain full control of my senses, and I always remained confused and puzzled for many minutes—my mental abilities in general, but especially my memory, were in a state of complete suspension.

In everything I suffered, there was no physical pain, but the emotional anguish was endless. My imagination became morbid, and I spoke constantly "of worms, of tombs, and epitaphs." I became lost in thoughts of death, and the fear of being buried alive took complete control of my mind. The terrible danger I faced haunted me both day and night. During the day, the agony of these thoughts was overwhelming—at night, it was even worse. When the dark night covered the earth, I would shake with every terrifying thought—trembling like the feathers on a funeral hearse swaying in the wind. When my body could no longer stay awake, I would fight against sleep—because I was terrified that when I woke up, I might find myself trapped in a grave. And when I finally did fall asleep, I would immediately enter a world of nightmares, where one overwhelming idea of death loomed over everything like a massive, black wing casting its shadow.

From the countless dark images that haunted my dreams, I choose to record just one vision. I believed I was trapped in a cataleptic trance that lasted longer and felt deeper than usual. Suddenly, an ice-cold hand touched my forehead, and an impatient, chattering voice whispered the word "Arise!" in my ear.

I sat up straight. The darkness was complete. I couldn't see the shape of whoever had woken me. I couldn't remember when I had fallen into the trance, or where I was lying. While I stayed still, trying to gather my thoughts, the cold hand grabbed me roughly by the wrist, shaking it impatiently, while the babbling voice spoke again:

"Get up! Didn't I tell you to get up?"

"And who," I demanded, "are you?"

"I have no name in the places where I live," the voice answered sadly. "I used to be human, but now I'm a demon. I was once cruel, but now I feel compassion. You can sense that I'm trembling. My teeth are chattering as I speak, but it's not because of the cold night—this endless night. This horror is unbearable. How can you sleep so peacefully? I can't rest because of these terrible cries of suffering. These sights are more than I can stand. Get up! Come with me into the darkness outside, and let me show you the graves. Isn't this a scene of misery?—Look!"

I looked, and the invisible figure that still gripped my wrist had caused all the graves of humanity to be thrown open. From each one came the dim, glowing light of decay, allowing me to see into the deepest chambers where I could observe the wrapped bodies in their sad and solemn sleep alongside the worms. But sadly, the true sleepers were outnumbered by many millions by those who could not sleep at all. There was weak struggling, a widespread sorrowful restlessness, and from the depths of the countless graves came a mournful rustling from the clothing of the buried. Among those who appeared to rest peacefully, I noticed that a great number had shifted, to varying degrees, from the stiff and uncomfortable positions in which they had originally been buried. And the voice spoke to me again as I stared:

"Isn't it—oh! isn't it a heartbreaking sight?" But before I could find the words to respond, the figure had stopped gripping my wrist, the glowing lights went out, and the graves slammed shut with sudden force, while from within them came a chaos of desperate cries, calling out again: "Isn't it—O, God, isn't it such a heartbreaking sight?"

These nighttime visions extended their terrifying influence well into my waking hours. My nerves became completely shattered, and I became consumed by constant horror. I was reluctant to ride, walk, or engage in any activity that would take me away from home. In truth, I no longer dared to venture beyond the immediate presence of those who knew about my tendency toward catalepsy, fearing that if I fell into one of my usual episodes, I might be buried before my true condition could be determined. I questioned the care and loyalty of my closest friends. I feared that during some trance lasting longer than usual, they might be convinced to consider me beyond recovery. I even went as far as worrying that, since I caused them so much trouble, they might welcome any particularly prolonged attack as adequate justification for disposing of me entirely. Their attempts to comfort me with the most serious promises were useless. I demanded the most sacred vows that under no circumstances would they bury me until decay had progressed so significantly that further preservation would be impossible. Even then, my deadly fears would not listen to logic and would accept no comfort. I implemented a series of detailed safety measures. Among other preparations, I had the family tomb redesigned to allow easy opening from the inside. The lightest pressure on a long lever extending deep into the tomb would cause the iron door to spring open. There were also arrangements for fresh air and light to enter freely, along with convenient storage for food and water within easy reach of the coffin meant for me. This coffin was lined with warm, soft padding and equipped with a lid designed like the tomb door, but with springs arranged so that even the weakest body movement would be enough to release it. Beyond all this, a large bell hung from the tomb's ceiling, with a rope designed to pass through a hole in the coffin and be tied to one of the corpse's hands. But sadly, what good is human vigilance against fate? Even these carefully planned safeguards were not enough to spare a soul already destined for these torments from the ultimate agony of being buried alive!

A time came—as it had many times before—when I found myself rising from complete unconsciousness into the first weak and unclear sense of being alive. Gradually— with the slowness of a tortoise—the faint gray dawn of mental awareness approached. A sluggish restlessness. An indifferent tolerance of dull pain. No concern—no hope— no struggle. Then, after a long stretch of time, a ringing sound in my ears; then, after an even longer pause, a prickling or tingling feeling in my hands and feet; then what seemed like an endless period of pleasant stillness, during which my awakening senses were fighting to become thoughts; then a brief sinking back into nothingness; then a sudden return. Finally the slight trembling of an eyelid, and immediately after that, an electric jolt of terror, deadly and unclear, which sends the blood rushing in streams from my temples to my heart. And now the first real attempt to think. And now the first effort to remember. And now a partial and fleeting success. And now my memory has regained enough control that I somewhat understand my condition.

I sense that I am not waking from normal sleep. I remember that I have suffered from catalepsy. And now, at last, as if struck by the force of an ocean, my trembling soul is crushed by the one terrible Danger—by the one ghostly and ever-present thought.

For several minutes after this thought took hold of me, I stayed completely still. But why? I couldn't find the courage to move. I didn't dare make the attempt that would reveal my fate—and yet something deep in my heart whispered that it already knew the truth. Despair—the kind that no other form of misery can create—despair alone drove me, after prolonged hesitation, to lift my heavy eyelids. I opened them. Everything was dark—completely dark. I understood that the episode had ended. I realized that the worst part of my condition had long since passed. I knew that I had fully regained the use of my sight—and yet everything remained dark—utterly dark—the complete and absolute darkness of an eternal Night.

I tried to scream, and my lips and dry tongue moved frantically together in the effort—but no sound came from my hollow chest, which felt crushed as if under the weight of an enormous mountain, gasping and throbbing along with my heart at every labored and desperate breath.

The movement of my jaw as I tried to scream showed me that it was tied shut, which is common practice with the dead. I also felt that I was lying on something hard, and my sides were tightly pressed by something similar. Up to this point, I hadn't dared to move any part of my body—but now I forcefully threw my arms upward, which had been stretched out with my wrists crossed. They hit a solid wooden surface that extended above me, no more than six inches from my face. I could no longer deny that I was lying inside a coffin.

And now, in the midst of all my endless suffering, sweet Hope arrived like an angel—because I remembered the precautions I had taken. I twisted and made frantic efforts to push open the lid: it wouldn't budge. I searched my wrists for the bell-rope: it couldn't be found. And then Hope abandoned me forever, while an even harsher Despair took complete control; because I couldn't ignore the fact that the padding I had so carefully arranged was missing—and suddenly, the strong distinctive smell of damp earth filled my nostrils. The realization was undeniable. I wasn't inside the vault. I had fallen into a coma while away from home—while among strangers—when or how, I couldn't recall—and they had buried me like an animal—sealed in some ordinary coffin—and pushed deep, deep, and forever, into some common and unmarked grave.

As this terrible realization forced its way into the deepest parts of my soul, I struggled once more to cry out loud. And in this second attempt I succeeded. A long, wild, and unending scream of agony echoed through the depths of the underground darkness.

"Hey! Hey there!" called out a rough voice in response.

"What the hell is wrong now!" said a second person.

"Get out of there!" said a third.

"What do you mean by howling in that kind of way, like a wildcat?" said a fourth person; and at that point I was grabbed and shaken roughly, for several minutes, by a group of very tough-looking men. They didn't wake me from my sleep—because I was completely awake when I screamed—but they brought back my full memory.

This adventure took place near Richmond, Virginia. I had gone on a hunting trip with a friend, traveling several miles down the banks of the James River. As night fell, we were caught in a storm. The cabin of a small boat anchored in the river, loaded with garden soil, provided our only available shelter. We made the best of the situation and spent the night aboard the vessel. I slept in one of only two sleeping berths on the boat—and the berths of a sixty or twenty-ton vessel hardly need description. The one I used had no bedding whatsoever. Its maximum width was eighteen inches. The distance from its bottom to the deck above was exactly the same. I found it extremely difficult to squeeze myself into the space. Despite this, I slept deeply, and my entire vision—for it was neither a dream nor a nightmare—arose naturally from my circumstances, my usual way of thinking, and the difficulty I mentioned of gathering my thoughts and especially recovering my memory for a long time after waking from sleep. The men who woke me were the boat's crew and some workers hired to unload it. The earthy smell came from the cargo itself. The bandage around my jaw was a silk handkerchief I had used to wrap my head, since I didn't have my usual nightcap.

The suffering I experienced was undoubtedly just as intense at the time as being buried alive would have been. The torment was terrifying—it was unimaginably horrible; but something good came from this evil, because the sheer intensity of it caused an inevitable change in my mind. My spirit gained strength—gained resilience. I traveled to different places. I exercised vigorously. I breathed the fresh air under the open sky. I focused my thoughts on topics other than death. I got rid of my medical books. I burned my copy of "Buchan." I stopped reading "Night Thoughts"—no more pompous writing about graveyards— no more frightening stories—like this one. In other words, I became a completely different person and lived a full life. From that unforgettable night onward, I permanently put aside my morbid fears, and along with them disappeared the cataleptic condition, which they had probably caused more than resulted from.

There are moments when, even to the rational eye of logic, the world of our troubled humanity may appear to resemble hell—but human imagination is not like Carathis, able to safely explore every dark corner. Unfortunately, the frightening army of death-related fears cannot be dismissed as purely imaginary—but, like the demons who accompanied Afrasiab on his journey down the Oxus River, they must remain dormant, or they will consume us—they must be allowed to stay asleep, or we will be destroyed.

The Domain of Arnheim

The garden was designed like a beautiful lady,
   Who appeared to be sleeping peacefully in joy,
And she closed her eyes to the open sky above.
   The blue expanse of Heaven was perfectly mirrored
   In a large circle, decorated with flowers of light.
The iris flowers, and the round drops of dew
That clung to their blue petals appeared
Like twinkling stars that sparkle in the evening blue.

—Giles Fletcher.

From birth to death, a wave of good fortune carried my friend Ellison through life. I don't use the word fortune merely in its material sense. I mean it as another word for happiness. The person I'm describing seemed born to demonstrate the theories of Turgot, Price, Priestley, and Condorcet—to prove through his own life what has been considered the impossible dream of those who believe in human perfection. In Ellison's short life, I believe I witnessed proof against the belief that somewhere in human nature lies a hidden force that works against happiness. A careful study of his life has led me to understand that generally, humanity's misery comes from breaking a few basic laws of human nature—that as a species we possess the unused ingredients for contentment—and that even now, despite the current confusion and foolishness in all thinking about society's great problems, it remains possible for an individual person, under certain rare and extremely lucky circumstances, to achieve happiness.

My young friend was completely filled with these same beliefs, and it's worth noting that the constant happiness that marked his life came largely from careful planning. It's clear that without the natural wisdom that sometimes serves as well as experience, Mr. Ellison would have been thrown by his remarkable success into the usual whirlpool of misery that awaits those with exceptional gifts. However, my purpose here isn't to write an essay about happiness. My friend's ideas can be summarized briefly. He believed in only four basic principles, or more precisely, requirements for true joy. What he considered most important was (surprisingly!) the simple and entirely physical matter of free movement in fresh air. "Health gained through other methods," he said, "hardly deserves the name." He pointed to the joy of fox hunters and drew attention to farmers, the only group of people who, as a whole, can truly be considered happier than others. His second requirement was the love of a woman. His third, and hardest to achieve, was rejecting ambition. His fourth was having a goal to pursue constantly; and he believed that, all else being equal, the amount of happiness one could reach depended on how spiritual this goal was.

Ellison was extraordinary in the endless stream of wonderful gifts that fortune showered upon him. In personal charm and beauty, he surpassed all other men. His mind was the type that found acquiring knowledge more like natural insight and essential need than hard work. His family ranked among the most distinguished in the empire. His bride was the most beautiful and loving of women. His wealth had always been substantial; but when he reached adulthood, it was revealed that one of those amazing twists of fate had worked in his favor—the kind that shock the entire social world where they happen, and rarely fail to completely transform the moral character of those who experience them.

It seems that roughly a hundred years before Mr. Ellison reached adulthood, a man named Mr. Seabright Ellison had passed away in a distant province. This gentleman had built up an enormous fortune, and since he had no close relatives, he came up with the unusual idea of letting his wealth grow for a full century after his death. He carefully and wisely planned out different ways to invest the money, then left the entire sum to the closest blood relative with the Ellison name who would still be living at the end of those hundred years. Many people tried to challenge this unusual inheritance, but since these attempts came after the fact, they failed. However, a suspicious government took notice, and eventually passed a law that banned all similar wealth accumulations in the future. This law, though, didn't stop young Ellison from inheriting his ancestor Seabright's fortune of four hundred and fifty million dollars when he turned twenty-one.

When word spread about the enormous wealth he had inherited, there were naturally many theories about how he might spend it. The sheer size and immediate availability of the fortune left everyone who considered it completely bewildered. Someone with any significant amount of money could be expected to do any number of things. With riches that simply exceeded those of other wealthy citizens, it would have been easy to imagine him indulging to extreme excess in the fashionable luxuries of his era—or involving himself in political scheming—or seeking ministerial power—or buying additional titles of nobility—or assembling vast collections of art and curiosities—or acting as a generous patron of literature, science, and the arts—or establishing and lending his name to extensive charitable institutions. But for the unimaginable wealth actually in the heir's possession, these pursuits and all conventional pursuits seemed to offer too narrow a scope. People turned to calculations, and even these only served to astound them further. They discovered that, even at three percent interest, the annual income from the inheritance totaled no less than thirteen million five hundred thousand dollars; which came to one million one hundred and twenty-five thousand per month; or thirty-six thousand nine hundred and eighty-six per day; or one thousand five hundred and forty-one per hour; or twenty-six dollars for every passing minute. This completely shattered the usual patterns of speculation. People simply didn't know what to think. Some even believed that Mr. Ellison would give away at least half of his fortune, considering it completely unnecessary wealth—enriching entire groups of his relatives by sharing his excess. To his closest relatives, he did indeed give away the considerable wealth that had been his own before the inheritance.

I wasn't surprised, though, to realize that he had already made up his mind about something his friends had debated endlessly. I also wasn't particularly shocked by what he had decided. When it came to personal acts of charity, he had put his conscience at ease. As for the possibility that people could actually improve the overall human condition through their own efforts, he had very little faith in that idea, I'm sad to say. Overall, whether for better or worse, he was largely left to rely on himself.

In the broadest and most noble sense, he was a poet. He understood, furthermore, the true nature, the magnificent goals, the supreme grandeur and dignity of poetic feeling. He instinctively felt that the fullest, if not the only proper fulfillment of this feeling lay in creating new forms of beauty. Certain peculiarities, either in his early education or in the nature of his mind, had colored all his moral thinking with what is called materialism; and it was this tendency, perhaps, which led him to believe that the most beneficial, if not the only legitimate field for poetic practice, lay in creating new moods of purely physical beauty. Thus it came to pass that he became neither musician nor poet—if we use this latter term in its everyday meaning. Or it might have been that he chose not to become either, simply in pursuit of his belief that in scorning ambition lies one of the essential principles of happiness on earth. Is it not indeed possible that, while a high level of genius is necessarily ambitious, the highest level is above what is called ambition? And might it not thus happen that many far greater than Milton have contentedly remained "mute and inglorious?" I believe that the world has never seen— and that, unless through some series of accidents driving the noblest type of mind into unwelcome effort, the world will never see—that full extent of triumphant achievement, in the richer realms of art, of which human nature is absolutely capable.

Ellison never became a musician or poet, even though no one lived with a deeper love for music and poetry. If his circumstances had been different, he might very well have become a painter. Sculpture, while poetic by nature, was too restricted in scope and impact to hold his attention for long. I've now covered all the areas where people commonly believe poetic feeling can flourish. But Ellison insisted that the richest, truest, and most natural field—if not the most expansive one—had been mysteriously overlooked. No one had ever described the landscape gardener as a poet, yet my friend believed that creating landscape gardens offered the ideal artist the most spectacular opportunities. This was truly the perfect arena for displaying imagination through endless combinations of new and beautiful forms, using elements that were far superior to anything else the earth could provide. In the countless varieties and colors of flowers and trees, he saw Nature's most direct and powerful attempts at physical beauty. By directing or focusing this effort—or more accurately, by adapting it for human eyes to appreciate—he realized he would be using the best possible approach and working most effectively to fulfill not only his own calling as a poet, but also the noble purposes for which God had given humanity the gift of poetic feeling.

"Its adaptation to the eyes which were to behold it on earth." In his explanation of this wording, Mr. Ellison did much to solve what has always seemed to me a mystery—I mean the fact (which only the ignorant dispute) that no such combination of scenery exists in nature as the painter of genius can create. No such paradises can be found in reality as have glowed on Claude's canvas. In the most enchanting of natural landscapes, there will always be found a flaw or an excess—many excesses and flaws. While the individual parts may challenge the highest skill of the artist, the arrangement of these parts will always be open to improvement. In short, no position can be reached on the wide surface of the natural earth from which an artistic eye, looking steadily, will not find something offensive in what is called the "composition" of the landscape. And yet how puzzling this is! In all other matters we are rightly taught to regard nature as supreme. With her details we shrink from competition. Who would dare to imitate the colors of the tulip, or to improve the proportions of the lily of the valley? The criticism which says, of sculpture or portraiture, that here nature is to be elevated or idealized rather than copied, is mistaken. No pictorial or sculptural combinations of points of human vitality do more than approach the living and breathing beauty. In landscape alone is the critic's principle true; and, having felt its truth here, it is only the reckless spirit of generalization which has led him to declare it true throughout all the domains of art. Having, I say, felt its truth here; for the feeling is no pretense or fantasy. Mathematics provides no more absolute proofs than the feelings of his art give the artist. He not only believes, but positively knows, that such and such apparently random arrangements of matter create and alone create true beauty. His reasons, however, have not yet been developed into words. It remains for a deeper analysis than the world has yet seen to fully investigate and express them. Nevertheless he is supported in his instinctive opinions by the voice of all his fellow artists. Let a "composition" be flawed; let a correction be made in its mere arrangement of form; let this correction be presented to every artist in the world; by each will its necessity be acknowledged. And even far more than this; to remedy the defective composition, each isolated member of the brotherhood would have suggested the identical correction.

I repeat that only in landscape arrangements can physical nature be elevated, and therefore, her ability to be improved at this single point was a mystery I had been unable to solve. My own thoughts on the subject had settled on the idea that nature's original intention would have arranged the earth's surface to fulfill at every point man's sense of perfection in the beautiful, the sublime, or the picturesque; but that this original intention had been disrupted by the known geological disturbances— disturbances of form and color—grouping, in the correction or soothing of which lies the soul of art. The strength of this idea was greatly weakened, however, by the necessity it involved of considering the disturbances abnormal and unsuited to any purpose. It was Ellison who suggested that they were prophetic of death. He explained it this way:—Accept that the earthly immortality of man was the first intention. We then have the original arrangement of the earth's surface adapted to his blissful state, as not existing but planned. The disturbances were the preparations for his later conceived mortal condition.

"Now," said my friend, "what we consider to be enhancement of the landscape might truly be such, but only from a moral or human perspective. Every change we make to the natural scenery could potentially create a flaw in the overall picture, if we imagine this picture being viewed as a whole—from a distance—from some point far from the earth's surface, though still within the bounds of its atmosphere. It's easy to understand that what might improve a detail when examined closely could simultaneously damage the general effect when observed from a greater distance. There might be a class of beings, once human but now invisible to humanity, to whom, from far away, our chaos might appear as order—our lack of beauty as beautiful; in other words, the earth-angels, for whose observation more than our own, and for whose death-refined appreciation of beauty, God may have arranged the vast landscape-gardens of the hemispheres."

During our conversation, my friend quoted several passages from a landscape gardening writer who is believed to have handled his subject matter quite well:

There are essentially two styles of landscape gardening: the natural and the artificial. The natural style aims to restore the original beauty of the countryside by adapting its methods to the surrounding landscape, growing trees that complement the hills or plains of the nearby land, and

32

discovering and implementing those subtle relationships of size, proportion, and color that remain hidden from casual observers but are apparent everywhere to the trained student of nature. The success of the natural gardening style is seen more in the elimination of flaws and inconsistencies—in the establishment of healthy harmony and order—rather than in creating any extraordinary wonders or spectacular displays. The artificial style offers as many variations as there are different preferences to satisfy. It maintains a general connection to various architectural styles. There are the grand avenues and secluded areas of Versailles, Italian terraces, and a diverse mixed old English style that relates to domestic Gothic or English Elizabethan architecture. Regardless of what criticism may be directed at the misuse of artificial landscape gardening, incorporating pure artistry into a garden setting greatly enhances its beauty. This appeals to the eye partly through the display of order and intentional design, and partly through moral sentiment. A terrace with an old moss-covered balustrade immediately brings to mind the elegant figures who once walked there in bygone eras. Even the smallest display of artistry serves as proof of care and human attention.

"From what I have already observed," said Ellison, "you will understand that I reject the idea, expressed here, of restoring the original beauty of the countryside. The original beauty is never as great as what can be created through human intervention. Of course, everything depends on choosing a location with potential. What is said about discovering and implementing subtle relationships of size, proportion, and color is one of those vague statements that serve to hide unclear thinking. The phrase I quoted could mean anything, or nothing, and provides no real guidance. The claim that the true result of natural-style gardening is seen more in the absence of flaws and inconsistencies than in creating special wonders or miracles is a proposition better suited to the limited understanding of ordinary people than to the passionate visions of a genius. The negative merit suggested belongs to that stumbling criticism which, in literature, would raise Addison to divine status. In truth, while the virtue that consists merely in avoiding vice appeals directly to the mind and can therefore be defined by rules, the higher virtue that burns in creation can only be understood through its results. Rules apply only to the merits of restraint—to the excellences that hold back. Beyond these, critical art can only offer suggestions. We may be taught to build a 'Cato,' but we are told in vain how to conceive a Parthenon or an 'Inferno.' Once the thing is done, however, the wonder accomplished, the ability to appreciate it becomes universal. The theorists of the negative school who, through their inability to create, have mocked creation, are now found to be the loudest in their praise. What, in its early stage as principle, offended their modest reason, never fails, in its mature accomplishment, to force admiration from their instinct for beauty."

"The author's observations on the artificial style," Ellison continued, "are less problematic. Adding elements of pure art to a garden scene greatly enhances its beauty. This is accurate, as is the reference to the sense of human interest. The principle he expresses cannot be disputed—but there may be something beyond it. There may be an objective that aligns with this principle—an objective that cannot be achieved through the means ordinarily available to individuals, yet which, if accomplished, would give the landscape garden a charm far exceeding what a sense of merely human interest could provide. A poet with exceptionally large financial resources might, while maintaining the essential idea of art or culture, or, as our author puts it, of interest, infuse his designs with such scope and innovative beauty that they would convey the feeling of spiritual intervention. It will become clear that, in achieving such a result, he gains all the benefits of interest or design, while freeing his work from the harshness or technical rigidity of worldly art. In the most rugged wilderness—in the most untamed scenes of pure nature—the art of a creator is evident; yet this art is apparent only upon reflection; in no way does it have the immediate force of an emotion. Now let us imagine this sense of divine design being brought down one level—being made somewhat harmonious or consistent with the sense of human art— forming a middle ground between the two: let us picture, for instance, a landscape whose combined vastness and precision—whose unified beauty, grandeur, and mystery, would suggest the idea of care, or cultivation, or oversight, by beings superior to, yet related to humanity—then the feeling of interest is maintained, while the art involved takes on the character of an intermediate or secondary nature—a nature that is not God, nor a direct expression of God, but which remains nature in the sense of being the work of angels that exist between man and God."

It was through dedicating his vast fortune to bringing such a vision to life—through the freedom of working outdoors under his personal supervision of the plans— through the constant purpose these plans provided— through the elevated spiritual nature of his goal—through the genuine disdain for ambition this allowed him to feel— through the endless sources of fulfillment that satisfied, without ever completely filling, his soul's greatest passion for beauty—and above all, through the companionship of a woman who remained truly feminine, whose beauty and love surrounded his life in the glorious atmosphere of Paradise, that Ellison believed he could find, and indeed did find, freedom from humanity's usual worries, along with far more genuine happiness than ever appeared in the ecstatic daydreams of De Staël.

I struggle to give readers a clear understanding of the amazing things my friend actually achieved. I want to describe them, but I'm discouraged by how difficult they are to explain, and I'm torn between going into specific details or speaking in general terms. Perhaps the best approach would be to combine both extremes.

Mr. Ellison's first step naturally involved choosing a location, and he had barely begun considering this matter when the lush beauty of the Pacific Islands caught his attention. In fact, he had decided on a voyage to the South Seas when a night of reflection convinced him to give up the idea. "If I were a misanthrope," he said, "such a place would be perfect for me. The complete isolation and seclusion, and the difficulty of getting in and out, would in that case be the greatest attraction; but I am not yet Timon. I want the peace but not the melancholy of solitude. I must retain some control over how long and how deeply I withdraw from the world. There will be many times when I will also need the understanding of those who appreciate poetry in what I have accomplished. Let me find, then, a place not far from a busy city—whose nearness will also best allow me to carry out my plans."

Looking for the perfect location, Ellison traveled for several years, and I was allowed to go with him. He quickly dismissed a thousand places that captivated me, for reasons that eventually convinced me he was correct. We finally reached a high plateau of remarkable richness and beauty, offering a sweeping view nearly as vast as that from Mount

Etna, and in both Ellison's judgment and mine, exceeding the famous vista from that mountain in all the genuine qualities of scenic beauty.

"I understand," said the traveler, letting out a deep, satisfied sigh after staring at this scene in wonder for almost an hour. "I realize that in my situation, nine out of ten of the most particular men would be perfectly satisfied here. This view is truly magnificent, and I would celebrate it if not for how overwhelming its magnificence is. Every architect I've ever encountered has the habit of placing buildings on hilltops for the sake of the 'view.' The mistake is clear. Grandeur in any form, but particularly when it comes to vastness, shocks and thrills us—then exhausts and discourages us. For an occasional sight, nothing could be better—for an everyday view, nothing could be worse. And when it comes to constant viewing, the most troublesome aspect of grandeur is its vastness; the most problematic part of vastness is its distance. It conflicts with the feeling and sensation of privacy—the feeling and sensation we try to satisfy when 'retreating to the countryside.' When we look out from a mountaintop, we can't help but feel exposed to the entire world. Those who are heartsick stay away from distant views like they would avoid a plague."

It wasn't until near the end of the fourth year of our search that we discovered a location that Ellison declared met his standards. Naturally, there's no need to reveal where this place was located. My friend's recent passing, which resulted in his estate being made accessible to particular groups of visitors, has brought Arnheim a type of mysterious and understated, if not reverent fame, comparable in nature but vastly greater in extent to the reputation that had long set Fonthill apart.

The typical way to reach Arnheim was by river. Travelers would depart the city in the early morning hours. Throughout the morning, they journeyed between shores displaying peaceful and charming beauty, where countless sheep grazed, their white wool creating spots of color against the brilliant green of gently rolling meadows. Gradually, the sense of human cultivation gave way to simple pastoral care. This feeling slowly transformed into an impression of seclusion, which then developed into an awareness of complete solitude. As evening drew near, the waterway grew narrower; the banks became increasingly steep; and these slopes were covered in lush, abundant, and darker vegetation. The water became more transparent. The stream curved and twisted in countless directions, making it impossible to see its shining surface for more than a furlong at any given moment. At every turn, the boat appeared trapped within a magical circle, surrounded by insurmountable and impenetrable walls of greenery, topped by a roof of deep blue satin, with no visible floor—the keel maintaining perfect balance on what seemed like a ghostly vessel that, somehow having been flipped upside down, traveled alongside the real boat as if to support it. The waterway now transformed into a gorge—though this term doesn't quite fit, and I use it only because our language offers no better word to describe the most remarkable, if not the most characteristic, aspect of this landscape. The gorge-like quality existed only in the height and parallel nature of the shores; all other features defied this description. The walls of this ravine, through which the clear water continued to flow peacefully, rose to heights of one hundred and sometimes one hundred and fifty feet, leaning so far toward each other that they largely blocked out daylight; meanwhile, the long, feather-like moss that hung thickly from the tangled shrubs above gave the entire chasm an atmosphere of somber gloom. The turns became more frequent and complex, often seeming to circle back on themselves, leaving the traveler completely disoriented. Furthermore, he found himself wrapped in an extraordinary sense of the mysterious. The concept of nature persisted, but her essence appeared transformed—there was an eerie symmetry, a captivating uniformity, an almost magical appropriateness in her creations. Not a single dead branch, withered leaf, loose pebble, or patch of bare brown earth could be seen anywhere. The crystal-clear water lapped against the pristine granite or the perfect moss with such sharp definition that it both delighted and confused the observer.

After navigating the winding passages of this waterway for several hours, with darkness growing deeper by the moment, a sudden and unexpected turn of the boat brought it abruptly into a circular basin of remarkable size compared to the narrow gorge they had just left, as if the vessel had been dropped from the heavens above. The basin measured roughly two hundred yards across and was enclosed on all sides except one—the opening directly in front of the boat as it entered—by hills that matched the height of the canyon walls, though they possessed a completely different character. The hillsides descended from the water's edge at approximately a forty-five-degree angle, and they were covered entirely from bottom to top—with not a single spot left bare—in a magnificent display of flowering blossoms, with hardly a green leaf visible among the vast sea of fragrant and shifting colors. This basin plunged to great depths, yet the water remained so crystal clear that the bottom could be seen distinctly in glimpses—composed of what appeared to be a dense layer of small, round alabaster stones—whenever the eye managed to look away from the reflected image of the blooming hills mirrored far below in the inverted sky. These slopes contained no trees or even large shrubs of any kind. The feelings stirred in anyone observing this scene were those of abundance, warmth, vibrant color, peaceful silence, perfect harmony, gentle softness, refined delicacy, graceful elegance, luxurious beauty, and an extraordinary level of cultivation that brought to mind visions of a new fairy race—industrious, refined, splendid, and supremely particular in their tastes; yet as the gaze followed the countless colored slope upward from where it met the water's edge to where it faded into the hanging clouds above, it became nearly impossible not to imagine a sweeping waterfall of rubies, sapphires, opals, and golden onyxes cascading silently from the sky.

The visitor, suddenly emerging into this bay from the dark ravine, feels both delighted and amazed by the complete circle of the setting sun, which they had assumed was already well below the horizon, but which now faces them directly, creating the only endpoint of an otherwise endless view seen through another canyon-like opening in the hills.

But here the traveler leaves the ship that has carried him this far and steps down into a light canoe made of ivory, decorated with intricate designs in bright scarlet, both inside and outside. The stern and bow of this boat rise high above the water with sharp points, giving it the overall shape of an irregular crescent. It rests on the surface of the bay with the elegant grace of a swan. On its white fur-lined floor lies a single feathery paddle made of satinwood, but no rowers or attendants can be seen. The guest is told to take heart—that fate will look after him. The larger ship vanishes, and he finds himself alone in the canoe, which appears to float motionless in the center of the lake. While he wonders what direction to take, however, he notices a gentle movement in the magical boat. It slowly turns itself around until its front points toward the sun. It moves forward with a gentle but steadily increasing speed, while the small waves it creates seem to splash against the ivory sides in heavenly music— seem to provide the only possible explanation for the soothing yet sad melody whose hidden source the confused traveler searches for around him without success.

The canoe moves forward steadily, and the rocky entrance to the vista draws near, allowing its depths to be seen more clearly. To the right rises a chain of tall hills that are roughly and abundantly forested. It can be noticed, however, that the characteristic of perfect cleanliness where the bank meets the water still continues. There is not a single sign of the typical river debris. To the left the nature of the scene is gentler and more clearly man-made. Here the bank rises upward from the stream in a very gradual slope, creating a wide expanse of grass with a texture that resembles nothing so much as velvet, and with a brightness of green that could compete with the color of the purest emerald. This plateau changes in width from ten to three hundred yards, extending from the riverbank to a wall fifty feet high, which stretches in endless curves while following the general path of the river, until it disappears in the distance toward the west. This wall consists of one continuous rock and has been created by cutting straight down through what was once the jagged cliff of the stream's southern bank, but no sign of this work has been allowed to remain. The carved stone shows the color of ages and is abundantly covered and draped with ivy, coral honeysuckle, eglantine, and clematis. The sameness of the wall's top and bottom edges is completely broken by occasional trees of enormous height, growing alone or in small clusters, both along the plateau and in the area behind the wall, but close to it, so that many branches (especially of the black walnut) extend over and lower their hanging ends into the water. Further back within the area, the view is blocked by an impenetrable barrier of leaves.

These observations occur as the canoe slowly moves toward what I've referred to as the entrance to the view. As we get closer to this point, though, the gap-like appearance disappears; a new passage from the bay becomes visible on the left side—where the wall can also be seen extending, continuing to follow the river's general path. The eye cannot see very far down this new opening; the stream, along with the wall, keeps curving to the left until both disappear completely behind the foliage.

The boat, however, glides effortlessly into the winding waterway; and here the shoreline across from the wall appears similar to the shore across from the wall in the straight view. Tall hills, sometimes rising into mountains and covered with wildly abundant vegetation, continue to enclose the landscape.

Drifting gently forward with slightly increasing speed, the traveler navigates through several short bends before discovering that his path seems blocked by an enormous gate—or more accurately, a door made of polished gold. The door features intricate carvings and decorative patterns, catching the direct light of the rapidly setting sun with such brilliance that it appears to set the entire surrounding forest ablaze. This gate sits within a towering wall that seems to stretch across the river at a perpendicular angle. Within moments, however, it becomes clear that the main current continues flowing in a gentle, sweeping curve toward the left, with the wall following alongside it as before.

Meanwhile, a substantial secondary stream branches off from the primary waterway, flowing with a soft murmur beneath the door before disappearing from view. The canoe enters this smaller channel and moves toward the gate. The massive doors slowly and harmoniously swing open. The boat glides through them and begins a swift descent into an enormous amphitheater completely surrounded by purple mountains, whose foundations are washed by a shimmering river that flows along their entire perimeter. At this moment, the complete Paradise of Arnheim reveals itself to the observer. A rush of captivating music fills the air; an overwhelming sensation of exotic, sweet fragrances pervades the atmosphere; the eye perceives a dreamlike blend of tall, graceful Eastern trees, dense clusters of shrubs, flocks of golden and crimson birds, lakes bordered with lilies, meadows filled with violets, tulips, poppies, hyacinths, and tuberoses, long interweaving lines of silver streams, and rising chaotically from the midst of it all, a structure of mixed Gothic and Saracenic architecture that appears to suspend itself miraculously in midair, sparkling in the red sunlight with countless bay windows, minarets, and spires, seeming like the ghostly creation of Sylphs, Fairies, Genies, and Gnomes working together.

THE END

Thank You For Reading

You've Just Read a Piece of the Greatest Library Ever Rebuilt

Thank you for reading.

This book is one of thousands we're restoring, reimagining, and translating as part of the **Modern Library of Alexandria** — a global movement to preserve and share humanity's most important ideas.

What was once lost to fire and time is now rising again — not just as memory, but as living, breathing knowledge, freely accessible to all.

What You Can Do Next:

- **Keep Reading.**

    Discover more legendary works — in beautiful print, audiobook, or digital form — at LibraryofAlexandria.com.

- **Build Your Own Library.**

    Every title is available as a paperback, hardcover, or collectible boxset — at true printing cost. Craft a personal library worthy of display.

- **Spread the Light.**

    Share this book. Tell others about the movement. Help us translate every timeless work into every language, so no reader is ever left behind.

By finishing this book, you've already taken part in something extraordinary.

Join us at LibraryofAlexandria.com

Together, we're rebuilding the greatest library the world has ever known.

With appreciation,

The Modern Library of Alexandria Team

Visit:
www.libraryofalexandria.com
Or scan the code below: